Effective Career Development

Advice for establishing an enjoyable career

Effective Career Development

Advice for establishing an enjoyable career

SARAH COOK

IT Governance Publishing

Every possible effort has been made to ensure that the information contained in this book is accurate at the time of going to press, and the publisher and the author cannot accept responsibility for any errors or omissions, however caused. Any opinions expressed in this book are those of the author, not the publisher. Websites identified are for reference only, not endorsement, and any website visits are at the reader's own risk. No responsibility for loss or damage occasioned to any person acting, or refraining from action, as a result of the material in this publication can be accepted by the publisher or the author.

IT Governance Publishing Ltd
Unit 3, Clive Court
Bartholomew's Walk
Cambridgeshire Business Park
Ely, Cambridgeshire
CB7 4EA
United Kingdom
www.itgovernancepublishing.co.uk

First published in the United Kingdom in 2022 by IT Governance Publishing.

ISBN 978-1-78778-378-2

FOREWORD

As this book illustrates, we need good cyber specialists at all levels. But in order to be successful in our cyber security careers, we need to focus on our soft skills as much as our technical capabilities. It's not just understanding the importance of passwords, firewalls and all the other technical stuff. It's also about working with others, project management, communicating clearly (verbally and written), being tenacious when we are right and being flexible when we need to be. These soft skills can be as difficult to develop as our technical skills.

As the technology and working world constantly change, the successful are those who are agile enough to embrace change.

I was interested in airline systems and so manoeuvred myself into that area for the most fulfilling part of my career. We cannot just sit back and let our careers control us. We're control experts and we need to take control of our own careers. This book sets out the career roadmap as a method for planning a route and being aware of how we have got to where we are in our careers.

It's relatively easy to update our technical skills with training, but developing our softer skills requires insight into who we are, changing our behaviours and adapting to new roles. This book will provide you with techniques and tools to help in this process. They are equally useful for those entering cyber, those leaving the area to take up other careers, and even for those retiring!

As my career progressed, I was responsible for the recruitment, onboarding and training of 400 IT/cyber risk managers of all levels. I wish I had this book with me then as the techniques and tools would have helped me immensely in helping them develop their careers.

May your career be successful, rewarding and fulfilling. It's your choice. "Make it so", and good luck with whatever career path you decide to pursue in the future.

Christopher Wright, author of:

- *Agile Project Management, Assurance and Auditing – A practical guide for auditors, reviewers and project teams*;
- *Fundamentals of Assurance for Lean Projects – An overview for auditors and project teams*;
- *Fundamentals of information Security Risk Management Auditing – An introduction for managers and auditors*;
- *How cyber security can protect your business – A guide for all stakeholders*; and
- *Reviewing IT in Due Diligence – Are you buying an IT asset or liability,* co-authored with Bryan Altimas.

For more information about Christopher's publications, please visit:
www.itgovernancepublishing.co.uk/author/christopher-wright.

PREFACE

This book is a practical guide to help you gain the skills and confidence to successfully develop your career.

Career development today is no longer a case of climbing the corporate ladder. The world of work has changed dramatically in the last decade and so have our expectations. Changing jobs, roles, locations, sectors and careers is becoming the new normal. A multidisciplinary career is no longer the exception.

The book will help you set career development objectives, recognise your achievements to date, build on your strengths and identify development opportunities. It includes exercises and activities to help you understand what is important to you in a job and how to attain your career goals.

By reading this book, you'll be able to assess the advantages and disadvantages of different career paths and set clear career development goals. I outline the role of mentoring in career development and how to build your personal brand, present yourself well online and in person, and find the resources you need to achieve your development goals. As an illustration, the book also provides a practical example of career development in the cyber security sector.

My hope is that you'll have an effective toolkit of strategies and techniques to develop a successful and happy career.

Sarah Cook

Managing Director, The Stairway Consultancy Ltd

www.thestairway.co.uk

ABOUT THE AUTHOR

Sarah Cook is the Managing Director of The Stairway Consultancy Ltd. She has more than 20 years' consulting experience, specialising in leadership and management development. Before this, Sarah worked for Unilever and as head of customer care for a retail marketing consultancy.

Sarah has practical experience helping managers and team members develop a successful and happy work life. She works as an executive coach to help individuals to effectively develop and manage their careers.

Sarah is a business author and has written widely on leadership, career and management development, team building and coaching. She also speaks regularly at conferences and seminars on these topics.

Sarah is a Chartered Fellow of the Chartered Institute of Personnel Development and a Chartered Marketer. She has an MA from the University of Cambridge and an MBA from The Open University. Sarah is an accredited user of a wide range of psychometric and team diagnostic tools.

For more information about The Stairway Consultancy, please see *www.thestairway.co.uk* or contact *sarah@thestairway.co.uk*.

Learn more about Sarah's other publications by visiting: *www.itgovernancepublishing.co.uk/author/sarah-cook*.

ACKNOWLEDGEMENTS

This book is based on best practice around creating and developing a successful career. The following organisations were valuable sources of reference:

Chartered Institute of Personnel and Development:
www.cipd.co.uk

National Careers Service
https://nationalcareers.service.gov.uk/

I would also like to thank the following reviewers for their helpful feedback during the production of this book:

- Chris Evans – Deputy Head of Service Architecture/Lead Service Architect;
- Alan Field – Managing Director;
- Rob Ford – Senior ITSM Consultant;
- Vicki Utting – Managing Executive of IT Governance Publishing and Vigilant Software; and
- Christopher Wright – Retired Director, Current ITGP Author.

DISCLAIMER

All names quoted in this book are fictitious and have been presented for learning, understanding and explaining purposes only.

CONTENTS

Contents

CHAPTER 1: TAKING CONTROL OF YOUR CAREER

Introduction to career development

If you are reading this book, I suspect that you want some change in your career. It could be that you want to re-evaluate what's important to you in a job, or that you want to learn new things, self-improve and develop. It could be that you are seeking new opportunities or that you want to recognise and consolidate existing skills.

Expectations of career development have changed. Gone are the days when careers were clearly mapped out and career advancement was merely about climbing the corporate ladder. In the decades immediately after the Second World War, people tended to stay in the same company and type of role throughout their working life. After 40 years or so, they could be sure of their pension.

This is no longer the case. Globalisation, technological advancements and now the COVID-19 pandemic have meant that organisations have had to flex, restructure, downsize and embrace new ways of working. Employees are less likely to have a long-term relationship with one organisation. A multidisciplined career has become the norm. Yet at the same time, as the pension age increases, people need to work for longer.

Now the 'new normal' is to have multiple career paths with the focus on personal fulfilment and advancement rather than climbing the career ladder. A CIPD report from 2022, "Wellbeing at work", found that job satisfaction and work–

life balance are the most important factors to people when thinking about their working lives.[1]

Ambiguity and tension in the workplace as well as hybrid working patterns have led to the creation of new types of jobs, including interim, temporary, freelance, part-time, external, adjunct and contract roles. An example is the 'gig economy' where part-time freelance work opportunities mean that people have more flexible ways to make a living or to supplement their income. Rather than corporate careers, many people today have 'project careers'. This often means moving from one industry sector to another and doing a variety of roles with various time and place commitments.

Examples of the variety of today's career paths can be seen in four people I have coached recently:

1. A 30-year-old who has been made redundant 6 times already and is currently working on a fixed-term contract in the IT department of a large corporation.

2. A 60-year-old who began her career in a large global organisation, dropped out of corporate life to set up a guest house in France and now works 6 months a year as an interim and the rest of the year as an unpaid volunteer for a cancer charity.

3. A 50-year-old HR business partner who has always worked in the public sector – for the fire service, then

---

[1] CIPD. 12 April 2022. "Wellbeing at work". *www.cipd.co.uk/knowledge/culture/well-being/factsheet#gref.*

two local councils – and who, in her spare time, runs a private business with her partner selling party items.

4. A 45-year-old who was an IT director at a large corporation in her mid-30s and then dropped out of work to adopt a child, retrained as a teaching assistant, and now works as a consultant for a recruitment consultancy.

These people, and many like them, epitomise the variety of career development routes that individuals can take during their working lives. There are a myriad of choices and no right or wrong. As we will see, depending on your life stage and economic and social commitments, there are more opportunities for a 'project career' than ever before.

People can no longer expect stability in a job. For example, Generation Z (people born 1997 to 2010) are three times more likely to change jobs, while baby boomers (people born between 1946 and 1964) had just two jobs on average in the past decade.[2]

Working time has also become increasingly fluid. The sophistication of technology means that businesses are no longer limited to specific geographical locations to manage their workforce, enabling people to work remotely.

---

[2] Heitmann, Blair. 11 October 2018. "The Job-Hopping Generation: Young Professionals Are On The Move." *https://blog.linkedin.com/2018/october/11/the-job-hopping-generation-young-professionals-are-on-the-move*.

The number of people working from home rose through necessity during the COVID-19 pandemic, with home working an important part of business continuity. Many experts believe that post COVID-19, the world of work will change further. Offices will still exist but as places of collaboration, idea exchanges and innovation. Hybrid working[3] will be the norm for most employees most of the time. Office visits will be limited to several days a week for team meetings, events, and check-ins with managers. Indeed, a 2020 Gartner survey revealed that 74% of CFOs and finance business leaders planned to keep their previously on-site workforce working remotely post COVID-19.[4] Many organisations are also adopting four-day weeks to improve work–life balance.

Personal responsibility

Previously, when career success was dictated by the choices you made in your 20s and your job and career were fixed for life, there was less emphasis on taking personal responsibility for your career development.

---

[3] Hybrid working is a model of flexible working where employees work partly in the physical workplace, and partly remotely – at home or from another workspace.

[4] Lavelle, Justin. 3 April 2020. "Gartner CFO Survey Reveals 74% Intend to Shift Some Employees to Remote Work Permanently". *www.gartner.com/en/newsroom/press-releases/2020-04-03-gartner-cfo-surey-reveals-74-percent-of-organizations-to-shift-some-employees-to-remote-work-permanently2*.

The ambiguity and fluidity of today's work environment means there is constant change. Individuals need therefore to be more flexible, curious and open to new ideas.

In an article published on the Stanford Graduate School of Business' website, Loren Mooney uses a gardening analogy to describe the concept of 'repotting' your career.[5]

Just as plants that are repotted thrive and grow sturdier, moving and reshaping your career journey will make your work more engaging, meaningful and fulfilling. It takes courage and determination to 'repot', but the results are worth it.

How to use this book

This book provides you with a toolkit to help you manage your career development. It contains exercises and activities to increase your self-awareness so that you are better able to make career choices. You will also find tools to help you develop a plan of action to attain your career goals.

The book takes the following route:

---

[5] Mooney, Loren. 22 January 2014. "Is It Time to "Repot" Your Career?" *www.gsb.stanford.edu/insights/it-time-repot-your-career*.

Chapter 2: Understanding where you are now

To know where you want to go, you need to know where you've been and where you're starting from.

In this chapter, you'll find self-awareness activities that will help you recognise your strengths and development areas.

Chapter 3: Understanding what's important to you in a job

This chapter helps you identify your personal and work values, your ideal job and work environment as well as the non-negotiables.

Chapter 4: Career development opportunities

Here you'll learn how your life-stage can influence your career choices. You'll understand the options for your future career path.

Chapter 5: Creating career objectives

This chapter will help you set short- and long-term career development goals.

Chapters 6 to 9: Mentoring, promoting yourself, resources and networks

The final chapters provide examples and sources of information and support for your career development, including how to find a mentor, promoting yourself and networking. In the final chapter you'll find examples of career development in the cyber security sector.

Your career vision for the future

To begin your career development journey, I recommend a preparatory exercise called 'my career vision for the future'.

A career vision is a mental image of your future career. It's a picture of who you want to be, what you stand for and what you want to do in the future. Often called 'best possible self',[6] having a clear vision of yourself at your best is shown to have a strong motivational effect.

Answer the following questions either with words or drawings. There are no right or wrong answers. If you do not have a response right now, skip to the next question.

You'll be asked to return to this exercise later in the book.

---

[6] K.M. Sheldon and S. Lyubomirsky. 2006. "How to increase and sustain positive emotion: the effects of expressing gratitude and visualizing best possible selves", *Journal of Positive Psychology*, 1(2), pp 73–82.

1. Imagine yourself at work in the future. You are in your ideal job and you are happy and fulfilled. If you don't know what your ideal job is, focus on what it is that makes you or would make you happy and fulfilled at work, rather than the role itself. Set your own timescale for this picture, e.g. in six months, one year, five years, ten years.
2. Visualising yourself in this time and place, answer the following:

a) What are you doing at work?

b) What do you see around you?

c) What are other people saying about you?

d) How do you feel?

Consider your responses and create your career vision statement, which epitomises your best possible self at work. Write it in the present tense, e.g. 'I am' rather than 'I will'.

Here are some examples:

- 'I am a recognised expert in technical support, encouraging innovation and helping clients solve their technical problems.'
- 'I am a leader in my organisation, making a difference to the lives of people that work there and supporting our local community.'
- 'I am a university lecturer, helping my students to learn and develop while being the best parent I can be.'

Write your career vision statement in the box below:

My vision is:

CHAPTER 2: UNDERSTANDING WHERE YOU ARE NOW

To know where you want to go, you need to know where you come from

If you want a career change, I recommend taking stock of your career history and where you are now. Author Maya Angelou said:

> *"If you don't know where you've come from, you don't know where you're going."*

In this chapter you'll find four activities to help you become more aware of what your past career says about you, how satisfied you are with your life and career now, what your strengths are and your development areas. These activities will help inform your future choices.

Life-line exercise

The first exercise is called 'life-line'. It uses the analogy of a journey or a road of life, which can take many shapes. It invites you to consider where you have come from and the road you have travelled to date.

The exercise is in two parts. Please remember there are no right or wrong ways of drawing your life road or answering the questions.

Part 1: Drawing your life road

On a piece of paper, draw a road that represents your life and career to date. This could be any type of road – a motorway, a main road, a lane or a side road. It may be straight in some parts and twisty in others. It may be clear or at times blocked. It might have side roads or dead ends. It may go up hills or down dales. Careers take many paths and at stages can feel like a blocked road. It is helpful to mark a line across the page as a happiness indicator (see figure 1 example).

Mark where you are now, then the events or happenings to date. Don't focus on work – what happens outside the workplace also impacts our career choices.

Part 2: Reflecting on the road you've taken so far

When you've finished your drawing, reflect on what the road says about your life and career so far. You may like to consider and record the following:

1. What the road you've travelled so far says about you as a person.
2. What elements characterise the high points in your life and career so far?
3. What elements characterise the low points in your life and career?
4. What appear to be the things that are crucial to you in your career and your life?

5. What other insights do you have on your career journey so far?

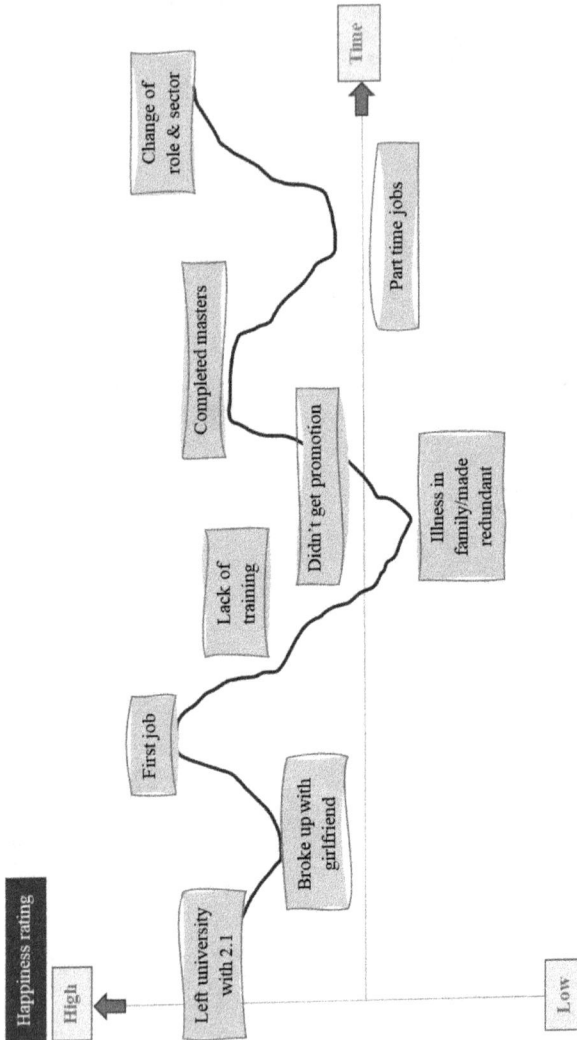

Figure 1: Example of a life road

Wheel of life activity

The next activity will also help you reflect on where you are in your life. The 'wheel of life' is a wheel with different spokes. Imagine this wheel reflects your life today and each spoke the key elements of your life.

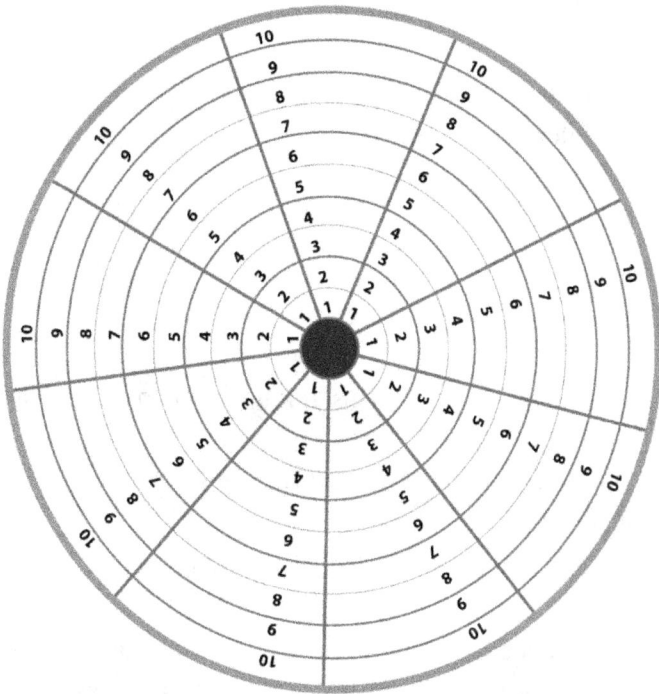

Figure 2: The wheel of life

The centre of the wheel (0) represents very dissatisfied and the outer edge (10) represents very satisfied.

Identify key areas of your life and title each segment accordingly.

Areas could be:

- Career
- Family
- Relationship with partner
- Children
- Friends
- Finances
- Personal development
- Health and fitness
- Social responsibility

But these are just suggestions. It is up to you to identify the areas relevant to your life.

Shade the segments to represent your satisfaction level with each area.

Once you have done this, take a moment to reflect on your scores and write some notes on the following:

a) What appear to be the things that are crucial to you in your life? (I.e., the labels you have given to each spoke.)

_____

b) Which are your highest scoring areas and why?

_____

c) Which are your lowest scoring areas and why?

_____

d) What does your wheel of life say about you as a person?

_____

Recognising your strengths

To move forward in your career, it's important that you recognise your strengths. These are things you excel at and how you add value to an organisation.

By recognising your strengths, you'll be able to play to them and better enjoy your time at work. Research by Gallup shows that people who use their strengths at work are six times more effective and engaged in their role.[7] You'll contribute more to the teams you work in and with, and open up new career opportunities.

People will hire you for the strengths you bring, so you need to be confident about talking about the things you are good at.

Some people find it difficult to recognise their strengths, or if they do, downplay them. When talking to others about your strengths, avoid vague words like 'maybe', 'probably', 'pretty much', 'quite' and 'generally'.

> *"My strength is **maybe** my ability to build strong relationships. **Probably pretty much** all my clients would agree I'm **generally quite** customer focused."*

Contrast this with:

> *"My strength is my ability to build strong relationships. All my clients agree I'm customer focused."*

So, what are your strengths, the attributes that make you really stand out?

You can identify these in three ways:

1. Complete the Table 1: Strengths Self-assessment analysis.
2. Ask for feedback at work from your manager, close colleagues and team, using questions like *'what are*

---

[7] Sorenson, Susan. "How Employees' Strengths Make Your Company Stronger". *www.gallup.com/workplace/231605/employees-strengths-company-stronger.aspx*.

my best attributes at work?' and *'where do I most add value in this project?'*.

3. Ask people you value outside work such as family and friends *what three words they would use to describe you.*

By contrasting your own and others' responses, you'll build a picture of your own natural talents and abilities.

Example:

Michaela, an IT manager, recently completed this activity and identified the following:

"I am naturally a good listener, I'm analytical and logical.

When I sought feedback from my boss and close colleagues, they described my best attributes at work as being 'quietly determined', 'a great executor', 'thorough' and 'reliable'.

I also asked my family and friends for feedback on the three words they'd use to describe me. The words they used were 'caring', 'good listener', 'funny', 'perceptive', 'logical' and 'always there to support'.

I was pleased with the feedback, and it reinforced the perception I have of my natural talents and the value I offer others at work."

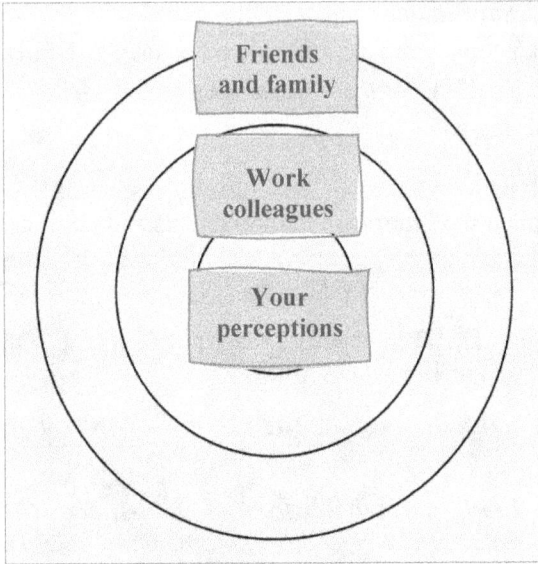

Figure 3: Identifying strengths

Self-assessment strengths exercise

Your strengths are a mixture of innate talent and things you've learned (sometimes called transferable skills). Learned strengths come from knowledge and experience and the behaviours we bring to work.

On the next pages you'll see a list of strength words. Tick those that apply to you. (You can add others to the list if they don't appear here.)

When you've completed the list, review the strengths you have chosen. Think about which are your most valuable qualities. Generally, these will be those that have bought you sustained success and which you most enjoy demonstrating.

Give each strength you have identified a score on a scale of 1 (low) to 10 (high).

Pick your three highest-scoring strengths and write them below:

1._____

2._____

3._____

Table 1: Strengths Self-assessment

Strength	Yes	No
Accuracy		
Adaptability		
Analysis		
Authenticity		
Calmness		
Caring for others		
Curiosity		
Change management		
Coaching		
Communication		
Coordination		
Creativity		
Determination		

Strength	Yes	No
Developing others		
Discipline		
Enthusiasm		
Evaluation		
Experience		
Focus		
Honesty		
Implementation		
Inclusiveness		
Independence		
Insight		
Leadership		
Listening		
Logical		

Strength	Yes	No
Mental arithmetic		
Motivation		
Networking		
Objective		
Ownership		
Organisation		
Patience		
Persuasion		
Persistence		
Positivity		
Problem-solving		
Project management		
Resilience		
Relationship management		

Strength	Yes	No
Research		
Responsible		
Selling		
Strategic		
Supportive		
Teamwork		
Time management		
Trustworthiness		
Versatility		

Identifying development areas

You've focused on strengths, but what about development areas? When you recognise your weaknesses, you can learn how to develop and give the best of yourself at work. However, a word of caution: we have a tendency, which starts from childhood, to focus on weaknesses and make them the focus of our attention rather than building our strengths.

Our strengths energise us and motivate us to achieve success. When we are playing to our strengths, we often lose track of time as we are focused and 'in the flow'.

My advice is to adopt the 80/20 rule. Focus 80% of the time on your strengths and how to demonstrate and build these, and only 20% of the time on your weaknesses.

Also, make sure you have a realistic plan of action to overcome each weakness.

For example, I was working with a manager who described their main weakness as 'not being good with detail'. She recognised that this was a recurring issue and would always be a weak point. Her mitigating action was to ensure that she had a good assistant on her team who could help her focus on the detail.

List two of your key personal development areas. As with your strengths, you may wish to ask for feedback from colleagues, family or friends:

1. _____

2. _____

For each development area, outline either a development opportunity or a mitigating action that will help you improve.

Reflection and action points from this chapter

Understanding where you've come from, your career road and choices to date can inform your future career path.

It's helpful to see your job and career in relation to your other life choices such as your family and friends, health, finances, etc.

Our key strengths are where we bring most value to an organisation – now and in the future.

As we come to the end of this chapter, consider when you last used one of your key strengths and the impact this has had.

CHAPTER 3: WHAT IS IMPORTANT TO YOU IN A JOB?

What is important to you in a job?

Having assessed where you have come from and where you are now, the next step is to identify what's important to you in a job.

In this chapter you'll find activities to help you identify:

- Your personal values;
- Your ideal work environment; and
- The non-negotiables.

These activities will help you to better understand your career priorities.

Case study: Kai's personal values

Kai worked in the head office of a major bank. It was a fast-paced and competitive environment where long hours and presenteeism were the norm.

Kai was promoted on several occasions and four years later he was headhunted by another financial services organisation. Here he headed a special project team. The work ethic meant that Kai left home early in the morning and arrived home late at night. He found it increasingly exhausting, Furthermore, his social life was restricted to weekends and he found it hard to stay in contact with his friendship group.

During one Christmas break, feeling washed out and reluctant to continue the same trajectory in the new year, Kai reflected on his personal values and what was important to him at work. He knew that helping others and making a difference were two of his key values but did not think these sat well with his job in financial services.

He decided to begin job hunting in the public sector and not-for-profit organisations, which he believed would better suit his personal values and lead him to feel happier and more satisfied at work and in his home life.

Identifying your personal values

Values are internal anchors or reference points that serve as moral principles for how we lead our lives. Our values and beliefs drive our behaviour, preferences and priorities. They are the lens through which we reference what is right and wrong, good and bad.

Identifying your personal values and what you hold dear is a useful exercise in self-understanding. When we are feeling stressed or frustrated at work it is often because our personal values are called into question.

Look back at your life-line road activity from the last chapter and consider when you were at your best – what was the work environment like? What were the underlying principles that were at play?

The list on the next two pages gives a wide range of values that may help you pinpoint what is important to you. Feel free to add any other values you may think of. Then, tick the things that are most important to you. Look to highlight eight key values.

Achievement	Cooperating with others	Excellence
Adventure	Creativity	Excitement
Challenge	Development	Expertise
Change	Democracy	Fast pace
Competence	Development	Flexible working hours
Competing with others	Ecology	Freedom
Contact with others	Effectiveness	Friendships
Having a family	Managing others	Responsibility
Helping people	Meaningful work	Routine
Honesty	Money	Security

Independence	Openness	Sense of community
Influence	Order	Serenity
Integrity	Personal development	Stability
Involvement	Physical challenge	Status
Job location	Power	Taking risks
Knowledge	Pressure	Tranquillity
Lack of pressure	Privacy	Truth
Leadership	Promotion	The environment
Love	Recognition	Variety
Loyalty	Relationships	Wisdom
Making decisions	Reputation	Working alone/working with others

Detail what these eight priorities mean to you. This will help you to identify and measure when these values are being met.

1. _____

2. _____

3. _____

4. _____

5. _____

6. _____

7. _____

8. _____

Consider:

- Which of the values are the most important to you? (You may need time to reflect on your list and to test and refine this.)

Then consider:

- How closely does your work environment fulfil these values?
- How important is it that your personal life and organisation reflect these values?

- What do you want to do if either your personal life or work life are not fulfilling these values?

Your ideal work environment

Having established your work values, the next activity invites you to build on this understanding and to imagine your ideal work environment. To do this, you'll also need to refer back to the vision you created in chapter 1.

This is a creative fantasy exercise and there are no right or wrong answers.

Visualise your ideal work environment, thinking about your vision and your values, then write down or draw the environment.

Here are two people's descriptions of their ideal work environment as examples:

- Working in a highly energised team, having variety, opportunity for fun, learning new things and having flexibility over child cover.
- A place that appreciates talent and gives me a chance to shine, to lead a team and to influence and where I have the choice of where I work (office or home).

Your ideal work environment:

[blank box]

The non-negotiables

Now think about what your envisioned ideal work environment says about what you are not prepared to accept in a job.

Here are some examples:

- Working five days a week in the office.
- Working in a highly competitive environment.
- Travelling away from home.
- Having to do lots of overtime.

List your non-negotiables here:

Reflection and action points from this chapter

Defining your personal values and what's important to you in a job requires time and reflection. The exercises in this chapter are intended to help you identify:

- **Your values:** what do you stand for?
- **What's important to you in a job:** what will motivate you and help you give of your best?

I recommend revisiting your notes from this chapter later to see if what you have written still resonates.

CHAPTER 4: CAREER DEVELOPMENT OPPORTUNITIES

Where do you want to go in the future?

In this chapter, I aim to help you better understand how your life stage influences your career choices. I'll also outline the options for development so that you are able to evaluate the advantages and disadvantages of each potential career path.

Your life stage and how this influences career choices

Our career choices take place within the context of society, the economy and our social setting. Each generation grows up in a different context and, as a result, tends to have different work expectations.

Here is a broad description of the characteristics of each of the six generations. This is based on trends and general social patterns identified by sociologists:

The Silent Generation
(typically born between 1925 and 1945):

This age group in their late 70s, 80s and 90s does not like to 'make a fuss' and therefore is sometimes called the Silent Generation. Traditionalist in their approach, the Silent Generation respects hierarchy and authority. They tend to be stoical and often communicate indirectly to avoid being critical of the existing order. There are few left of this generation in the workplace.

The Baby Boomers
(typically born between 1946 and 1964):

Baby Boomers grew up in a booming post-war economic climate of regeneration and growth. Task focused and achievement oriented, this generation has worked hard – often at the expense of their private lives. Moving towards retirement or semi-retirement, many are still in work either full time or part time. This generation aims to live a fulfilling life in their later years.

Generation X
(typically born between 1965 and 1980):

Brought up by work-orientated Baby Boomers, Generation X are often called 'latch-key kids' and they grew up to be self-reliant. Impatient and goal oriented, they want to work hard and have the freedom to make their own decisions.

Generation Y
(typically born between 1981 and 1996):

Generation Y, or Millennials as they are generally known, are (at the year of publication: 2022), aged between 23 and 40. They value development and expect to be quickly given opportunities at work as well as the flexibility to act. Generation Y are always connected and online. This means that they are sociable and community aware. They challenge authority and are less likely to stick to the rules than Generation X or Baby Boomers.

They seek work with a purpose and appreciate teamwork and collaboration. Career development is very important to them.

**Generation Z
(typically born after 1997):**

At the entry point of the workforce. They are highly networked and tech-aware. They appreciate organisations that promote diversity and inclusion. They are prepared to work independently, money and job security are important to them, and they prioritise a healthy work–life balance.

Age and your relationship with work

When you look at the descriptions of the generations, do any of these resonate with you?

In the workforce, we are likely to find a range of generations. A key learning point is that different things are important to people at different ages.

The following table typifies how what's important to us changes over time:

Table 2: Stages of Work Life

Stage of life	What is important
16–21 years: Setting off	• Establishing independence • Making own choices
21–29 years: The age of possibilities	• Selecting a career • Setting career goals • Establishing relationships
30–39 years: Becoming established	• Evaluating future career and life goals • Settling into work and home
40–45 years: Mid-life crisis	• Question and re-evaluate work and life achievements
45–55 years: Middle adulthood	• Acceptance of who you are, what you've achieved, and that time is finite
55–75 years: Maturity	• Enjoyment of here and now

Where are you in relation to this table? How well does this typify what's been important to you in your work and career so far?

Add your personal reflections here:

Understanding the options for development

There are lots of options when it comes to career development. The following pages outline the principal routes you can take.

You know best where you've come from, what you want to achieve and which option is the most suitable. Therefore, I suggest you consider the advantages and disadvantages of each option.

Upwards progression

Aspiring to move upwards in your current or a different organisation or sector can bring material success, greater responsibilities, potentially management and leadership opportunities and a sense of achievement.

Example:

After graduating, Joe started his work career as a trainee and has moved up the ranks as a programmer, then a supervisor, before leading a small team of developers. Now looking for his next career step, Joe is considering whether to try for a more senior management position.

When considering upward progression, what are the advantages and disadvantages for you personally?

Moving sideways

A further option is to stay in a role or position at a similar level but to move sideways. This can provide challenge and variety as well as opportunities for development and deepening of expertise. The sideways move does not have to be in the same organisation and may encompass different forms of employment, for example, consultancy, interim work, self-employment, projects.

Example:

Kiela has worked for three years in the same department. Feeling the lack of challenge but wanting to stay at the same level, this year she successfully applied to work for a customer service team. She had always received good feedback on her ability to develop customer relationships and found she had many transferable skills that suited the new role. Although the grade is the same as her previous role, the change of job and environment have energised Kiela.

When considering moving sideways, what are the advantages and disadvantages for you personally?

Staying where you are

One route to consider is staying in your current job. There may be opportunities to further enhance and develop your skills and experience. You may be satisfied and secure in your current job. However, watch out for complacency and that your confidence doesn't suffer.

Example:

Phill is well respected in his role and enjoys being an expert in his field. He likes the company he works for and enjoys working in his team. He works from home and likes the flexibility his employer affords around working hours. He can start work early and finish to help with childcare when his children need collecting from school.

When considering staying in your current role, what are the advantages and disadvantages for you personally?

Changing direction

Changing direction is an option where you seek a completely alternative career. For example, you may be an accountant and decide to retrain as a vet.

Example:

Sam has worked for ten years in IT and has always enjoyed the roles he has had. However, he decided last year to take a sabbatical to re-evaluate his career path.

Sam has always enjoyed art and was attracted by a more creative career. This year he has enrolled at university to

---

become a jeweller as he believes this change of role will bring him more fulfilment.

When considering changing direction, what are the advantages and disadvantages for you personally?

Moving backwards

In some situations, it could be pertinent to take on a lower-level role or to take on a job that suits your circumstances but for which you are over-qualified, or that pays less than your potential.

Example:

Siobhan is the mother of three young children. Her partner has a recently moved to a leadership role and works long hours. Siobhan decided to seek a job much below her previous pay grade. The organisation was a good fit with her values and provided a less pressured environment and shorter working hours. This works well for Siobhan given her family commitments.

When considering moving backwards, what are the advantages and disadvantages for you personally?

Stopping 'traditional' work

Sometimes called 'experimenting', for an increasing number of people, another route is stepping off the traditional work 'merry-go-round'. This can allow people time to stand back and reflect. Taking a sabbatical or break in employment is becoming more common, as is taking time out to look after children or to take on the role of carer as well as returning to education.

Example:

Sophie is a 38-year-old account director who has worked for different medium-sized organisations for nearly 20 years. Feeling increasingly stressed after the pandemic, Sophie has stopped work and is taking a three-month sabbatical while she decides whether to retrain in order to move into a different sector or to pursue her dream of working with horses.

When considering stopping traditional work, what are the advantages and disadvantages for you personally?

Reflection and action points from this chapter

I started this chapter by outlining how different life stages can influence our career choices. There are many different career routes, and many people have 'project careers'.

Take a moment to consider where you are in your life stage and which career option you favour. We will build on this in the next chapter.

CHAPTER 5: CREATING CAREER OBJECTIVES

You are now halfway through this book and I hope that you have a clearer picture of who you are, where you've come from and how you'd like your career to develop.

In this chapter, you'll have the chance to create short- and longer-term career goals. This will help you formulate a plan for taking the first steps in your career development. The subsequent chapters will help you to put your plan into action.

Self-coaching questions

On the following pages, there are some self-coaching questions. They are designed to help you reflect on and set career goals and action plans.

There are no right or wrong answers. If you can't answer a question, skip to the next one. Or think about what question you should be asking yourself here.

The purpose of the exercise is to help you set objectives and reflect on potential strategies to achieve these. You may find it helpful to write down your responses.

Aim

- What would you like to achieve overall in your career?
- Specifically, what would you like to be different?
- By when do you want to see a change? (Ensure this is a realistic time frame.)

- Given your overall goal, what is an achievable short-term career objective?
- What is a realistic timescale for achieving this?

Situation

- What is happening right now?
- On a scale of 1 to 10, where are you now in relation to your short-term career objective?
- How is this impacting you? In what ways?
- Who else is involved and what is their opinion of the situation?
- What else is relevant?

Experience

- What have you already tried to tackle the issue?
- What experience do you have of similar situations and how have you tackled them in the past?
- What lessons have you learned about obtaining your career goals?
- What have you seen others do in similar situations?

Strengths

- What strengths do you have to help you achieve your objective?
- What qualities do you have that you could use?

Resources

- Who or what can you turn to for guidance and support?
- What or who can inspire or nourish you?

Options

- What strategies could you adopt to achieve your objective?
- What other ideas and perspectives are there?
- If you were being the best you could be, what would your instinct tell you to do?
- If you could wave a magic wand, what solution would you come up with?

The way forward

- What different perspectives have you gained from this exercise?
- What specific actions can you now take?
- What is the very first step in achieving your objective?
- When and how will you take this?
- Who do you need to inform and when will you do this?
- What support do you need?
- How and when will you get that support?

Reflection and action points from this chapter

The process of self-coaching can help you clarify your overall career goals and set specific objectives. By imagining the first steps in the process of your plan of action you are more likely to start your journey to a future career.

Write down the actions you have decided on and set a calendar reminder to review your progress.

CHAPTER 6: MENTORING

Using the experience of others

One useful approach to help you develop in your career is to find a mentor. In this chapter, I outline what mentoring is, the role of a mentor and a mentee, how to find a mentor and how to prepare for a mentoring relationship.

What is mentoring?

Mentoring is a process where two people establish a trusted relationship in which one person (the mentor) provides guidance and assistance and shares their knowledge and experience to help the other person (the mentee) grow and develop their career.

In his seminal book *Everyone Needs a Mentor*, David Clutterbuck explains

> *"A mentor is a more experienced individual willing to share knowledge with someone less experienced in a relationship of mutual trust."*[8]

There are many examples of mentoring in the workplace. Mark Zuckerberg, Meta CEO, publicly named his mentor Steve Jobs, the former Apple CEO, as a key factor in his success.

---

[8] D. Clutterbuck, *Everyone Needs a Mentor*, CIPD Publishing, London, 2004.

American TV presenter Barbara Walters mentored international star Oprah Winfrey and helped her develop her career.

The role of the mentor

A mentor is typically someone inside or outside the organisation who:

- Helps the mentee set career development goals;
- Is available for the mentee and listens to them actively;
- Shares their experience and gives advice and guidance;
- Respects confidentiality;
- Encourages the mentee to be responsible for their career; and
- Inspires confidence and motivates the mentee to move forward.

The role of the mentee

For a mentoring relationship to work well, the mentee needs to:

- Be open about their needs;
- Be clear about their career aspirations and goals;
- Trust their mentor and heed their experience and advice;
- Agree specific actions with their mentee and put these into practice; and
- Take responsibility for their own learning.

Examples of mentoring in action

1. Ash works in organisational development. His ambition is to move into a senior management role. Ash has had a mentor for the past two years. She is a senior manager in Operations and brings experience of working in a different department as well as knowledge of what it takes to move up the career ladder. Ash touches base with his mentor every 8 to 12 weeks. She has helped him gain a wider perspective of the organisation as well as providing advice on diversity, change management and leadership.

2. Tanzi started her career in IT more than ten years ago and has held various positions as an employee, interim and consultant. She has had the same mentor for the past five years. He is the director of an IT consultancy and has supported Tanzi in her career choices and in improving her confidence.

3. Phillipa is new to management and values the experience of her mentor, Steve. Phillipa started her career in planning and after two years was promoted to supervisor. She has recently been promoted again, to manager. This is her first line management role. Phillipa is finding it hard to delegate and has had feedback that she is getting too involved in day-to-day detail. Regular meetings with Steve have helped her reflect on her role and understand how delegation

> will help her as well as developing her team members. It is early days, but already Phillipa is seeing higher levels of motivation in her team.

Finding a mentor

Should you feel that having a mentor would be beneficial, how do you go about finding one?

Some forward-thinking organisations have mentoring programmes, and it may simply be a case of you contacting the programme owner to ask them to help you find a mentor. If not, you'll need to be more proactive.

I suggest brainstorming the names of people you know or know of who are well respected and have more experience in your field. They can be inside or outside your organisation. Typically, they will be at a higher level than you, but this may not always be the case. Next, make a shortlist of possible mentors.

It will be up to you to contact a potential mentor to see whether they would be willing to take on the role. This does not have to be a 'formal' relationship, nor does it need to be long term. For example, you might be seeking advice around a specific project or task. From my experience, people are happy to share their experiences and give support and advice.

There is also a useful site, *https://findamentor.com/*, which offers a free mentor–mentee matching service. The site also provides resources and communities with which you can potentially link.

It can take time to find the right mentor, so don't be put off if your first request is turned down. Persevere as you will eventually find a suitable mentor.

Making mentoring work

Here are some tips on making the mentoring relationship work.

Be prepared:

- Reflect on your reasons for wanting a mentor and what you want in your career development.
- Be ready to tell your mentor specifically what you want to achieve.
- Discover as much as you can about your mentor, for example their career history and their online presence.
- Be prepared to discuss with them how they can help you.
- Before the first meeting, send your mentor a brief introduction to yourself and your own career history.
- Think about where your meetings will take place, for how long and at what intervals.

When meeting your mentor for the first time:

- Be clear what you would like from the relationship. It's you who drives the agenda.
- Take time to explain your career to date and ask questions to better understand your mentor's career journey.

- Be open and honest with your mentor. The relationship needs to be based on trust.
- Discuss the challenges you face to achieve your goals and seek your mentor's advice.
- Agree specific actions you will take and timelines. Agree when you will meet again.
- As a record of your meeting, follow up with a summary email.

During subsequent meetings:

- Update your mentor on your progress, what you've achieved, what has gone well and what issues you have faced.
- Seek feedback from your mentor and advice for future actions.
- Share your next steps.
- Review your mentoring relationship at regular intervals to ensure that you are both happy with its progress.

Reflection and action points from this chapter

Mentoring is a proven method for helping individuals in their career development.

Take a few moments to consider who may be a good mentor for you.

A further consideration is whether you could be a mentor. Mentoring can be mutually beneficial. It can be a great opportunity for you to build your confidence and help others develop.

CHAPTER 7: PROMOTING YOURSELF

Throughout this book I've encouraged you to take personal responsibility for your career. In this chapter, we'll look at what you can do to promote yourself so that you achieve your career goals. I'll discuss what can stop you getting what you want, how to build your self-confidence and develop your personal brand as well as using tools such as LinkedIn to promote yourself as well as tips for preparing a 'stand-out' CV.

Self-confidence assessment

To develop your career, you need to believe in yourself, recognise your successes and trust your abilities.

Use the following assessment to evaluate your levels of self-confidence.

Table 3: Self-confidence Assessment

	Agree strongly	Agree	Disagree	Disagree strongly
1. I find it easy to recognise my successes				
2. I respect myself and				

	Agree strongly	Agree	Disagree	Disagree strongly
feel I am a person of worth				
3. I trust my own abilities				
4. I take a positive approach towards my achievements				
5. I am satisfied with who I am				
6. I often compare myself unfavourably with others				

	Agree strongly	Agree	Disagree	Disagree strongly
7. At times I feel I'm a failure				
8. I find it difficult to believe in myself				
9. I put myself down in front of others				
10. I feel I have no good qualities				

How to score

For statements 1 to 5, score:

- 4 points – Agree strongly
- 3 points – Agree
- 2 points – Disagree
- 1 point – Disagree strongly

For statements 6 to 10, score:

- 4 points – Disagree strongly
- 3 points – Disagree
- 2 points – Agree
- 1 point – Agree strongly

Now total your score.

Scores between 31 and 40: You have a great deal of confidence in yourself. This will help you to promote your successes and drive your career forward.

Scores between 21 and 30: You have medium levels of self-confidence. Look at which your low-scoring areas and consider how this impacts your approach to career development. Read the following pages for tips and advice on improving your self-confidence.

Scores between 10 and 20: You have low levels of self-confidence. Your ability to progress in your career may be hampered by your own limiting self-beliefs. Read the following pages for tips and advice on how to build your confidence.

Barriers to career development

There are things in life we have little influence over, such as world events and the economy. However, in our immediate sphere of influence, we all have the capacity to achieve most of our goals, given the right skills and qualifications.

Often the biggest barriers to us achieving our career goals are the beliefs we hold about ourselves. One of the reasons we suffer from lack of confidence is because we allow too many negative thoughts, which can create feelings of failure and rejection. Our beliefs can block and limit our progress and make us fearful of change.

Typical limiting beliefs around careers include:

- 'It's safer to stick to what you know'
- 'I'm not capable of change'
- 'It's too difficult for me to learn new skills'
- 'I can't move because of my family circumstances'
- 'The right job will come along in the end'
- 'I'm not a credible candidate'
- 'My experience is too limited'

Consider your own limiting beliefs. Now challenge yourself as to whether these are true, and consider how you can begin to overcome these barriers. Read on for tips and advice.

Career development approaches

When it comes to developing your career, there are four approaches you can take: :

1. Accept and make the most of the situation

For some people, accepting and making the most of your current work situation is a suitable career strategy. It's about appreciating what you already have, , enhancing the positives and minimising the negatives. It could be, for example, that you decide to stay where you are and focus more on other aspects of your life, spend more time with your family and develop more outside interests.

2. Change the current work situation

If you feel stuck in your career, the answer is not always to quit your job. It's easy to blame others and wait for them to notice and give you what you need.

Consider what's hindering you at work. What can you do to change the situation? This could involve taking on a new project, asking for a pay rise, influencing your boss or changing your working practices to give your role a reboot.

3. Change yourself

Consider how you can change yourself to make things better. For example, you could learn new skills, alter your behaviour, adjust your expectations or change your lifestyle so that you feel more fulfilled.

4. Leave

The last option involves moving on from your current situation. This could be getting a new role, changing industries or taking time off.

Whatever option you choose, you'll need to have confidence and self-belief to act.

Developing self-confidence

Here are some simple exercises to help build self-confidence.

Practical activities for increasing your self-confidence

1. Write a positive letter of affirmation

- Write a list of statements about yourself that you know are true – you need at least six statements.

- Write them in the present tense using positive language.

For example:

1. "I am a systematic and logical thinker"
2. "I am a confident speaker"
3. "I am a great problem-solver"

Keep this list of positive affirmations with you at work and read them twice a day until you memorise them. Repeat the phrases to yourself during any stressful situation to alleviate your anxiety.

2. Avoid comparing yourself to others

People with low self-confidence tend to compare themselves to others and consider themselves less able or less experienced. They may have self-doubt and feel they are not worthy of their position, that soon they will be 'found out'. Sometimes called 'imposter syndrome', this can put an individual's happiness and well-being at risk.

To avoid this, reframe how you think about others. If you see someone who is good, for example, at speaking up in meetings, think 'what can I learn from this person?', rather than 'I'll never be good at that'.

Focus on the things that are going well in your life and that you are grateful for. I find writing a 'gratitude list' very helpful in this respect. Each day, write down one or two things that you appreciate. This can be anything that resonates with you, e.g. 'The view of the sunrise from my window this morning' or 'My sister sending me a WhatsApp message to see how I am'. When you find your own contentment, you are less likely to compare yourself to others.

3. Confidence starts at home

If you lack self-confidence, you'll often find it hard to recognise your strengths and talk about your needs. This will probably be as much the case at home and with friends as with colleagues and your manager at work.

A safe place to begin building your confidence is by talking about your achievements with friends and family. Speak about small successes and things you are proud of; it doesn't have to be work related, e.g. a nice meal you cooked or a walk you took with friends. The important thing is finding your voice and feeling comfortable about articulating your contribution to something. The more you practice this at home, the easier it will become to speak up about your strengths in a work environment.

4. Visualise yourself being successful

The ability to see yourself doing things well acts as a program for the mind to put those steps into action – the unconscious mind cannot differentiate between fact and fiction![9]

To visualise success, think of an occasion or situation where you do not feel confident, e.g. presenting in front of a certain group of people.

---

[9] Hamilton, David. 30 October 2014. "Does your brain distinguish real from imaginary?" *https://drdavidhamilton.com/does-your-brain-distinguish-real-from-imaginary/.*

Close your eyes and imagine yourself being successful. Watch yourself doing what you want to happen.

Consider:

- Where you are;
- Who is with you;
- What you are saying and doing;
- How you look – how you are dressed and the gestures you use; and
- The positive reactions from others to what you are saying and doing.

Play this over several times in your mind, making the picture clearer and clearer each time. Notice the physiological changes as you do and how much more positive you feel about the event.

Do this before any situation where you need to be confident.

5. Positive self-talk

This activity will help you become more aware of your emotions and self-talk, using two contrasting situations: one where you are confident and the other where you lack confidence. This will highlight the need for positive self-talk to be confident.

First, think of a recent occasion where you felt confident. Answer the following questions:

- What was happening?
- What were you saying to yourself about the situation (your self-talk)? What tone did your self-talk have?

What kind of language were you using?

- What physical sensations and feelings were you aware of?
- What was the outcome of the situation?

Next, think of a recent occasion where you did not feel confident. Answer the following questions:

- What was happening?
- What were you saying to yourself about the situation (your self-talk)? What tone did your self-talk have? What kind of language were you using?
- What physical sensations and feelings were you aware of?
- What was the outcome of the situation?

Compare your reactions to the two situations. Think about the actions you can take the next time you lack confidence and answer the following questions:

1. What positive statement could I say to myself to be reminded of my strengths and achievements?
2. What could I do that would help me feel differently?
3. What could I do differently next time I am in this situation?
4. What self-talk or actions would empower me?

Building your personal brand

According to a 2020 study, almost all employers (98%) do background research on candidates online. Most HR professionals (72%) say a résumé is very important when evaluating an applicant. Almost all employers (95%) consider an "elevator pitch" important.[10]

To stand out from the crowd, therefore, candidates need a tailored, professional online and offline presence. This means creating a 'personal brand', a unique identity that shows your value to potential employers. Like a commercial brand, a personal brand sets out who you are,

the values you embrace and the way you express those values.

To create your own personal brand, here are some questions to ask yourself:

- What do you want to be known for? I.e. what do you want people to say about you when you are not in the room?
- What do you stand for?
- What motivates you?
- What situations energise you?
- What characteristics are you most complimented on?
- How can you reinforce your personal brand?

In answering these questions, and considering who your audience is, you can create an 'elevator pitch' about yourself.

---

[10] McKeon, Kelsey. 28 April 2020. "5 Personal Branding Tips For Your Job Search". *https://themanifest.com/digital-marketing/5-personal-branding-tips-job-search.*

Creating an elevator pitch

Most employers consider an "elevator pitch" important.

Sometimes called a 'personal statement', this is a short summary of your personal brand that is condensed enough to fit into the length of an elevator (lift) ride – a 30 to 60 second statement about who you are. Effectively, it is a reduction of the essential components of your brand – who you are, what you stand for and what you can offer.

If you have not done so already, I strongly recommend developing an elevator pitch.

You can use your personal brand to promote yourself via LinkedIn, CVs and interviews. Your elevator pitch or personal statement will also help you in these situations.

Using LinkedIn

According to a 2020 study by *The Manifest*, a business news and how-to website, most employers (90%) factor a job candidate's social media accounts into their hiring decisions, and79% have rejected a candidate based on their social media content.[11]

LinkedIn is the most used global recruitment tool. The platform now boasts more than 830 million members in more than 200 countries.[12]

---

[11] McKeon, Kelsey. 28 April 2020. "5 Personal Branding Tips For Your Job Search". *https://themanifest.com/digital-marketing/5-personal-branding-tips-job-search*.

[12] *https://about.linkedin.com/*.

It is important that you think strategically about how you want people to perceive you and your personal branding online. Most people have a LinkedIn profile, but many people don't complete all the sections. It is important to do this as it gets you more attention.

Here are some key tips to best optimise your LinkedIn profile:

- Look at the profiles of people you know and compare with your own.
- Search for your name on LinkedIn – is it easy to find? You can edit your profile URL so that it contains just your first name and surname rather than numbers. If your name is difficult to pronounce, make use of the name pronunciation feature on LinkedIn, which allows you to record how to pronounce it. You can also use this feature to record a personal message about yourself.
- Use a high-quality professional photo for your profile picture. To ensure search engines can find your profile, click on your photo and choose the option of showing the photo either to 'All LinkedIn Members' or 'Public'.
- Use the profile headline and the 'About' section to fully describe your expertise, who you are, where you add value, what you stand for. This is the 'landing' section for your audience, so use interesting and descriptive language to attract the visitor and showcase your personal brand.

- Fill in your work history and education. Remember to highlight key projects and achievements. If you've had a long career, it's best to only list the most recent 10 to 15 years.
- Fill in the skills section. It's helpful to have endorsements from other people, and for you to endorse others. This is because when you endorse someone on LinkedIn, the endorsement goes both on your and their profile. Recruiters search for people who are endorsed by others. They also search by industry groups, so it is useful if you belong to relevant groups.
- Post online, comment on others' posts and add links to your profile – the more activity you have, the higher your social networking score.

Creating an impactful CV

The 2018 Recruiter Study also found that nearly three out of four recruiters (72%) say a good CV is very important when evaluating an applicant.

Each job post can receive up to 250 applications. The principal way that recruiters sort through CVs is via an applicant tracking system (ATS). This software scans applications to find key words linked to the job description.

A tip is to identify the key words in the description of the position you are applying for. Incorporate these in the descriptions of your own achievements and experience on your CV, including in your personal statement. Matching as many keywords as you can will help recruiters locate your profile. This means you need to 'tweak' your CV and cover letter to each potential job application.

Here are some when tips when preparing your CV:

Write clearly and authentically; avoid flowery language.
Avoid tables, graphics and boxes, which can confuse the ATS.
Include a personal statement at the beginning of your CV that sums up your personal brand and relates to the key words in your desired post.
List your roles in chronological order, starting with your most recent post. However, don't just provide a list of duties. State your experience and achievements, using strong action words such as 'built', 'created', 'improved', 'solved'.
Focus on your strengths and how you add value. Wherever possible, back up your achievements with facts and figures, e.g. 'increased sales revenue by 8%', 'generated efficiency savings of £500,000'.
Limit your CV to two pages. If you have had a long career, this may mean condensing your earlier roles and giving more prominence to the most relevant experience.
Tailor your strengths and accomplishments from each of your past roles to the job you are applying for.

If you haven't got the exact experience required, focus on your transferable skills, e.g. communication, negotiation, project management, team leadership, etc.

Put your educational qualifications towards the end of your CV.

Add personal interests and out-of-work activity such as volunteering or personal projects that illustrate your personal brand.

Reread your CV, checking the formatting and layout for readability and, importantly, making sure there are no spelling mistakes.

When your CV is ready, write a one-page cover letter. Don't make this a copy of your CV. Highlight what makes you qualified for the role and how you'll bring value to the organisation. In a cover letter, you have opportunity to show your passion for the job and to tell a story.

Dos and don'ts in presenting yourself at interview or assessment centres

If you are called for interview, ensure that you research the company beforehand.

Know your CV well and prepare examples of your achievements relating to the job and desired behaviours. Think SARR: situation, action you took, results and relevance (to the role).

If, as sometimes happens, you are asked to deliver a presentation on a topic, make sure that you rehearse this beforehand and that you stick to time.

Prepare questions that you can ask people interviewing you. If you have not taken part in an interview for some time, it's helpful to have a trial run with a colleague or friend.

It's also best practice to ask for feedback after the interview. This can help highlight what you did well and any improvements for the future.

Reflection and action points from this chapter

In this chapter I set out tips and techniques for improving your self-confidence and presenting yourself in the best possible light, both online and in person.

If you have not done so already, I recommend writing down your personal brand as well as developing an elevator pitch.

CHAPTER 8: SOURCES OF INFORMATION

Whatever route you decide on to further your career, you'll probably need more information, as well as help from other people to achieve your goals. In this chapter, I'll help you consider how you may do this.

Identify the gaps

There are many places you can go for help in developing your career. Before you begin, it is important to first identify what you are missing. What are the gaps in your knowledge, skills or experience?

For example, if you want to take on a leadership role, what experience do you have? What skills have you acquired to date? What knowledge do you have of how to become a leader? What are the competencies you may need to develop?

How do you like to learn?

Once you have identified the gaps, consider how you like to learn:

- What are the best ways to increase your knowledge, skills or experience?
- What development training do you feel you may benefit from and why?
- In what specific ways do you think your current role can help prepare you for the future you desire?

- What types of other experiences do you think would help you develop?
- Where or from whom might you best gain that experience?

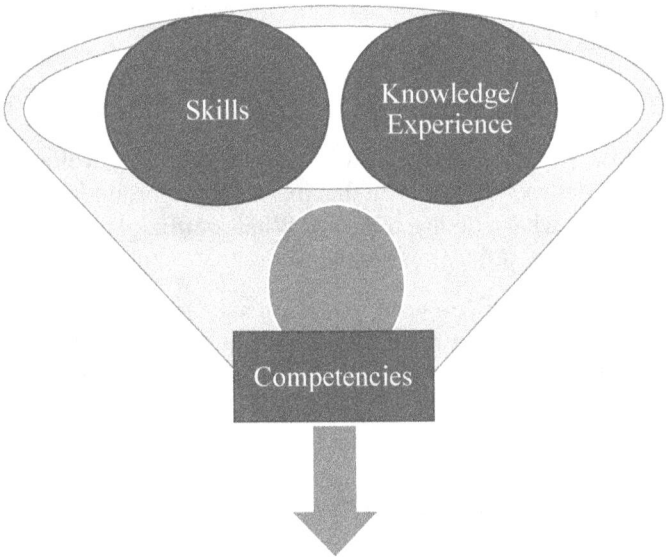

Figure 4: Identify the gaps

70/20/10 model of learning

It's helpful also to consider how we learn. The 70/20/10 model states that people obtain 70% of their knowledge from job-related experiences, 20% from social interactions with others, like co-workers and managers, and 10% from formal learning events.

The diagram on the following page illustrates a range of options that can help your development, either as structured learning, learning from others or learning from experience.

Sources of help

There are a wide variety of people you can turn to for help and support.

Family and friends

I recommend speaking to your family and friends about your career aspirations. They can be a useful sounding board and a listening ear. They may also be able to provide you with contacts or know of job openings. Recently a colleague helped her son find a placement via a friend. Another colleague who wanted to change career direction found helpful advice from a friend who worked in her desired field and who she first met at her local gym.

Table 4: 70/20/10 Learning

		• Increasing scope or responsibility • Taking on a new project • Onboarding a new team member • Being a mentor • Taking on a high-stakes, high-visibility assignment
	• Practice • Ongoing feedback • Coaching	
• E-learning/remote learning • Classroom workshops • Conferences and seminars • Literature reviews • Professional organisation membership	• Action learning sets • One-to-one discussions • Communities of practice • Being mentored • Review meetings	• Tackling a persistent, unresolved problem • Doing a cross-functional project • Networking and community volunteering

10% structured learning	20% learning from others	70% learning from others

Your manager

Whether you want to move upwards, sideways or to a different role, develop your personal competencies or become more of a technical expert or a leader, your manager can be a useful source of help and advice. Discuss your career development at your one-to-ones and ask for their support.

A mentor

In chapter 6, I discussed the benefits of mentoring and how to find a mentor. Mentors provide guidance and advice around career development based on their experience.

HR and learning and development

If you find it hard to speak to your manager or believe they are not supporting you in your career aspirations, it can be useful to have a discussion with your HR or learning and development team about the options available. Look out for job posts and development opportunities. Most organisations offer development training and some also provide sponsorship around external qualifications, so it is worth investigating what is on offer within your organisation.

Research experts in the field

If you want to change industry sectors or develop your expertise in your desired field, find out who the thought leaders are and follow the experts. Go online and look for people who are successful in their field, what they have published, their social media posts, etc. This is a helpful way of understanding current issues and future trends. You can also reach out to them for information, as described below.

Industry bodies

Likewise, research what industry bodies or trade associations exist for your area. Most sectors have a professional body or association that provides membership and qualifications and can be a useful source of information, career advice and development. Some larger organisations even have secondment opportunities.

Networking

Actively grow your network. It's important to expand your connections and develop your professional circle to widen your visibility. The people you network with may not be offering a job, but in connecting with them, you develop your personal brand and can learn from them.

Look out for conferences and seminars you can attend either virtually or face to face. LinkedIn groups where like-minded individuals connect and share information are also a good source of contacts.

When you connect with people, look for opportunities to seek advice. For example, you can ask:

- How do you see the industry growing?
- What qualifications and experience do you see as essential?
- How do you stay up to date with trends?

- Are there any associations or network circles I should join?

Most people are happy and often flattered to be asked for advice. Don't be shy about reaching out to others. You may suggest an informal chat over coffee or a short online call, email exchange or LinkedIn contact to start the process.

Remember too that networking is a two-way street. You can be a useful source of information for others, so be prepared to give as well as take.

And if you think that networking is not for you, be bold, not passive! A 2016 LinkedIn survey found that 85% of critical jobs are filled via networking of some sort.[13]

Volunteering and work experience

If you want to know what a job or industry is really like, look for opportunities to get experience, for example via shadowing or interim work.

If you are not able to connect directly with people in your desired industry, look for volunteering opportunities where you can develop your skills. For example, perhaps there is a local not-for-profit organisation that would benefit from volunteers with IT or marketing skills, or where you can practise your leadership skills.

---

[13] Adler, Lou. 29 February 2016. "New Survey Reveals 85% of All Jobs are Filled Via Networking". *www.linkedin.com/pulse/new-survey-reveals-85-all-jobs-filled-via-networking-lou-adler?*.

Test-driving a job first, be it directly or indirectly, can help you determine the skills and experience that are required as well as seeing whether you're making the right career move.

Identify who you need to influence and sources of information

Although you are responsible for your own career development, you will need help and support to achieve your development goals.

To conclude this chapter, I recommend brainstorming to identify the gaps in your career development, how to find information about filling these gaps, who you need to ask for help and how you will do this.

CHAPTER 9: EXAMPLE: CAREER DEVELOPMENT IN THE CYBER SECURITY SECTOR

In this chapter I focus on the cyber security industry, illustrating the career development paths and options available in this sector. I outline the different entry points and career options and provide an example of career development in this growing marketplace.

The cyber security industry

If you have chosen or are thinking of selecting cyber security as a career, you'll be working in a marketplace where there is high demand for talent. According to the UK Cyber Security Council cyber security covers *"all aspects of how individuals and organisations reduce the risk of cyberattack"*.[14]

Cyber security is one of the world's most pressing challenges. Cyber threats impact critical infrastructure, national security, the global economy and society. CB Insights's "Cyber Defenders 2021" report identified 14 technical categories of cyber security, including growing marketplaces such as automotive security.[15] The report identified a lack of dedicated cybersecurity staff, with 22%

---

[14] *www.ukcybersecuritycouncil.org.uk.*

[15] *www.cbinsights.com/reports/CB-Insights_Cyber-Defenders-2021.pdf.*

of companies reporting significant shortage and 42% a slight shortage. The high demand for talent is predicted to grow as the world of work, post COVID-19, moves to higher levels of hybrid and remote working, which brings with it increased risk of cyber attacks.

Roles in cyber security

There are many opportunities for people to start and to develop their careers in cyber security. A useful resource is CyberSeek (*www.cyberseek.org/pathway.html*), which provides an interactive career pathway for cyber security roles. It shows entry and transition opportunities and gives detailed information about the credentials and skillsets required for each role as well as the salary levels. Feeder roles for cyber security include:

- Networking
- Software development
- Systems engineering
- Financial and risk analyst
- Security intelligence
- IT support

The following table provides a brief overview of roles and career development paths.

Table 5: Example: Career Development in the Cyber Security Sector

Entry-level roles	Mid-level roles	Advanced roles
Cyber security specialist	Cyber security analyst	Cyber security manager
Cyber crime analyst	Cyber security consultant	Cyber security engineer
• Incident and intrusion analyst • IT auditor	Penetration and vulnerability tester	Cyber security engineer

Note that as the cyber security industry is growing and constantly evolving, you may see different categories or titles depending on the company or resource you use.

The good news is that there are very many career options. The three principal routes for career patterns tend to fall into:

1. Developing technical expertise
2. Security management and governance
3. Leadership

1. As a technical expert, this career route can cover, but is not limited to security engineering, identity access management, security operations, ethical hacking, Cloud security.
2. The security management and governance career path typically includes audits and compliance, training and awareness, third-party risk management and project management.
3. Leadership encompasses roles such as chief privacy officer and chief information security officer as well as managing and directing domains. These types of career paths are more people-focused.

Another key consideration is whether to apply for roles in-house as part of an internal security team or to work in the outsourced managed security sector. There are many start-ups and entrepreneurial firms that are expanding the specialisms in the managed security sector.

Useful resources

A useful resource is the UK Cyber Security Council.[16] The Council provides information on careers and development opportunities. In the US, there is the Cybersecurity and Infrastructure Security Agency (CISA).[17]

---

[16] *www.ukcybersecuritycouncil.org.uk/*.

[17] *www.cisa.gov/about-cisa*.

If you are new to the cyber security sector, the UK Cyber Security Council website sets out routes into the industry such as cyber security apprenticeships[18], free online resources and development opportunities, including qualification and training options.

The membership body ISACA® also provides cyber security qualifications and accreditation to suit all levels, from beginner to practitioner to manager to decision maker.[19]

The body is also a useful source of information and insights. For example, in his December 2021 ISACA blog,[20] Dr Jack Freund, VP and Head of Cyber Risk Methodology at security vendor BitSight, predicted the three skills for success in cyber security in 2022:

1. Cyber risk quantification – *"the process of evaluating the cyber risks that have been identified and then validating, measuring and analysing the available cyber data using mathematical modelling techniques".* In other words, maths capability and analysis skills are very important.

---

[18] *www.instituteforapprenticeships.org/apprenticeship-standards/?keywords=cyber.*

[19] *www.isaca.org/training-and-events.*

[20] *www.ukcybersecuritycouncil.org.uk/news-insights/news/isaca-reveals-the-skills-we-ll-need-for-2022/.*

2. Executive presence – cyber security professionals need the soft skills to present to and influence senior executives competently and confidently.
3. The ability to 'learn how to learn' – with large-scale innovation and change predicted in the cyber security sector, the ability to learn and relearn is critical.

Career examples in the cyber security sector

After achieving a BA in Computer Science at Loughborough University, Beth began her career in IT support, where she undertook her Microsoft Professional Certification.

During this time, Beth had a mentor who advised her to look at the expanding cyber security industry as her next career move. In her own time, Beth completed a further qualification (Information Systems Certification) online. This helped her secure a cyber security specialist role at a managed security organisation.

Now 28 and having worked since she left university, Beth is planning to take a year's sabbatical to go travelling and work as a volunteer for a charity overseas. She wants to come back to the industry and is debating whether her next steps should be to deepen her technical expertise or to move into a people management role.

She believes her time as a volunteer where she will be leading a small group of people will help her in her decision.

Beth is not certain of coming back to the same role in the industry on her return. She is considering looking for project work or an interim role after her sabbatical if a full-time position does not immediately become available as work–life balance is important to her.

Mark is a chief information security officer for a major insurance company.

Having undertaken a degree in technology, Mark joined a well-known IT consultancy where his roles focused on project management of major software integration programs.

Taking a new job in the US, Mark broadened his knowledge of the cyber security field by becoming a Certified Cloud Security Professional (CCSP).

With an ongoing interest in business and people development, he worked in cyber security for a major retailer before undertaking a master's degree in cyber security and information assurance.

Moving back to UK, he worked for a time as a consultant in the cyber security sector, expanding his network as well as undertaking a professional qualification in coaching.

He landed the job of chief information security officer a year ago and sees his key skills in the C-suite as leadership, communication and influencing, and financial fluency.

Key learning points

You may already work in cyber security or be thinking about moving into the field – or you may know very little about it. Whatever your level of cyber security expertise, I have used the cyber security industry as an example of career development opportunities as I feel it epitomises that successful career development is about having the following mindset:

Being self-driven

Successful cyber security professionals take the initiative and are self-driven.

Change ready

As the world of cyber security moves quickly and constantly, innovation and collaboration skills are increasingly important to help people be change ready.

Development oriented

The speed of technological change means that people in this sector need to learn and adapt quickly.

CHAPTER 10: CONCLUSIONS AND ACTIONS

The era of multidirectional careers

In an time where jobs for life are a thing of the past, moving regularly between roles, organisations, industries and locations is now the norm.

To successfully navigate the changing world of work, you need to take ownership of and be passionate about your own development.

Key learning points

To best develop your career, it is important to:

1. Reflect on where you have come from and what you have achieved.
2. Recognise your strengths, transferable skills and development areas.
3. Know what's important to you (your values).
4. Understand how your age, generation and life stage impacts your career development choices.
5. Have a vision of your future career and set yourself short- and long-term career objectives.
6. Consider how mentoring can help you progress your career.
7. Build your self-confidence to positively present your strengths and value.

8. Create a strong personal brand online, in writing and face to face.

9. Identify your development gaps, the best way to fill these and who you can turn to for help and support.

10. Learn how to learn and be flexible in the face of change.

Actions you can take now

Look back over your notes and reflections from the exercises and activities in this book.

Now list the tips and actions you can help you further your career.

Write your top three actions in the box below:

Top 3 actions:
1.
2.
3.

To ensure that you move forward in your career, prioritise the action you will take first. Think about how you will do this, when and who you need for support. As Abraham Lincoln said: *"The best way to predict the future is to create it."*

Good luck in your future career!

"*If you can dream it, you can do it.*"

Walt Disney

"*Success is a journey, not a destination.*"

Arthur Ashe

"*You can't build a reputation on what you're going to do.*"

Confucius

"*I've failed over and over again in my life. And that is why I succeed.*"

Michael Jordan

FURTHER READING

IT Governance Publishing (ITGP) is the world's leading publisher for governance and compliance. Our industry-leading pocket guides, books, training resources and toolkits are written by real-world practitioners and thought leaders. They are used globally by audiences of all levels, from students to C-suite executives.

Our high-quality publications cover all IT governance, risk and compliance frameworks and are available in a range of formats. This ensures our customers can access the information they need in the way they need it.

Our other soft skills publications include:

- *Well-being in the Workplace –A guide to resilience for individuals and teams* by Sarah Cook, *www.itgovernancepublishing.co.uk/product/well-being-in-the-workplace*
- *Making a Success of Managing and Working Remotely* by Sarah Cook, *www.itgovernancepublishing.co.uk/product/making-a-success-of-managing-and-working-remotely*
- *Building a High-Performance Team – Proven techniques for effective team working* by Sarah Cook, *www.itgovernancepublishing.co.uk/product/building-a-high-performance-team*
- *Changing how you manage and communicate change – Focusing on the human side of change* by Naomi

Karten,

www.itgovernancepublishing.co.uk/product/changing-how-you-manage-and-communicate-change

For more information on ITGP and branded publishing services, and to view our full list of publications, visit *www.itgovernancepublishing.co.uk*.

To receive regular updates from ITGP, including information on new publications in your area(s) of interest, sign up for our newsletter:

www.itgovernancepublishing.co.uk/topic/newsletter.

Branded publishing

Through our branded publishing service, you can customise ITGP publications with your company's branding.

Find out more at

www.itgovernancepublishing.co.uk/topic/branded-publishing-services.

Related services

ITGP is part of GRC International Group, which offers a comprehensive range of complementary products and services to help organisations meet their objectives.

For a full range of GCR International Group's resources, visit *www.itgovernance.co.uk/*.

Training services

The IT Governance training programme is built on our extensive practical experience designing and implementing management systems based on ISO standards, best practice and regulations.

Our courses help attendees develop practical skills and comply with contractual and regulatory requirements. They also support career development via recognised qualifications.

Learn more about our training courses and view the full course catalogue at *www.itgovernance.co.uk/training*.

Professional services and consultancy

We are a leading global consultancy of IT governance, risk management and compliance solutions. We advise businesses around the world on their most critical issues and present cost-saving and risk-reducing solutions based on international best practice and frameworks.

We offer a wide range of delivery methods to suit all budgets, timescales and preferred project approaches.

Find out how our consultancy services can help your organisation at *www.itgovernance.co.uk/consulting*.

Industry news

Want to stay up to date with the latest developments and resources in the IT governance and compliance market? Subscribe to our Weekly Round-up newsletter and we will send you mobile-friendly emails with fresh news and features about your preferred areas of interest, as well as unmissable offers and free resources to help you successfully start your projects. *www.itgovernance.co.uk/weekly-round-up*.

EU for product safety is Stephen Evans, The Mill Enterprise Hub, Stagreenan, Drogheda, Co. Louth, A92 CD3D, Ireland. (servicecentre@itgovernance.eu)